Smithsonian

LITTLE EXPLORER

TYRANNOSAURUS REX

by A. L. Wegwerth

CAPSTONE PRESS
a capstone imprint

Little Explorer is published by Capstone Press,
1710 Roe Crest Drive, North Mankato, Minnesota 56003
www.capstonepub.com

Library of Congress Cataloging-in-Publication Data
Wegwerth, A. L., author.
Tyrannosaurus rex / by A.L. Wegwerth.
pages cm. — (Smithsonian little explorer. Little paleontologist)
Summary: "Introduces young readers to Tyrannosaurus rex,
including physical characteristics, diet, habitat, life cycle, and the
Cretaceous period"— Provided by publisher.
Audience: Ages 4–7.
Audience: grades K to 3.
Includes index.
ISBN 978-1-4914-0810-0 (library binding)
ISBN 978-1-4914-0816-2 (paper over board)
ISBN 978-1-4914-0822-3 (paperback)
ISBN 978-1-4914-0828-5 (eBook PDF)
1. Tyrannosaurus rex—Juvenile literature. 2. Dinosaurs—Juvenile
literature. I. Title.
QE862.S3W44 2015
567.912'9—dc23   2014007845

Editorial Credits
Kristen Mohn, editor; Heidi Thompson, designer; Wanda Winch,
media researcher; Kathy McColley, production specialist

To my Bug and my Bear —A. L. W.

Our very special thanks to Mike Brett-Surman, PhD, Museum
Specialist for Fossil Dinosaurs, Reptiles, Amphibians, and Fish at
the National Museum of Natural History, Smithsonian Institution,
for his curatorial review. Capstone would also like to thank Kealy
Wilson, Product Development Manager, and the following at
Smithsonian Enterprises: Ellen Nanney, Licensing Manager;
Brigid Ferraro, Vice President, Education and Consumer
Products; Carol LeBlanc, Senior Vice President, Education
and Consumer Products.

Image Credits
AP Images: Museum of the Rockies, 10; Capstone: James Field, 1,
13 (middle), Steve Weston, 11; Corbis: 17 (bottom left), Stocktrek
Images/Mark Stevenson, 14-15, 28-29, Visuals Unlimited, 27 (b);
Dreamstime: Cmindm, 22-23, Elena Duvernay, 18-19 (Trex); Getty
Images Inc: Photo Researchers/Mark Hallet Paleoart, 20-21; Photo
Researchers/Richard Ellis, 6 (blue whale); Illustration by Karen
Carr, 8-9; iStockphotos: JonathanLesage, 26 (left); Jon Hughes,
cover; Luis V. Rey, 27 (top); Newscom: SOLO Syndication/Mark
Large, 17; Robert DePalma, 14 (bottom left, right); Shutterstock:
Alexonline, 26 (r), andrea crisante, 2-3, BACO, 4 (bus), Bob Orsillo,
13 (b), Burben, 29 (mr), Computer Earth, 30-31, DM7, 16, 19 (br),
ducu59us, 18-19 (bkgrnd), leonello calvetti, 12, nmedia, 29 (m),
Photobank gallery, 4-5, puchan, 29 (mr), Ralf Jurgen Kraft, 6 (br),
25 (m), reallyround, 5 (br), Sofia Santos, 4 (bl), 6-7, Steffen Foerster,
5 (bl), T4W4, 4 (t); Scotese, C.R., 2002, http://www.scotese.
com, (PALEOMAP website), 10 (map); SuperStock: National
Geographic, 24-25

Printed and bound in the United States of America.
009807R

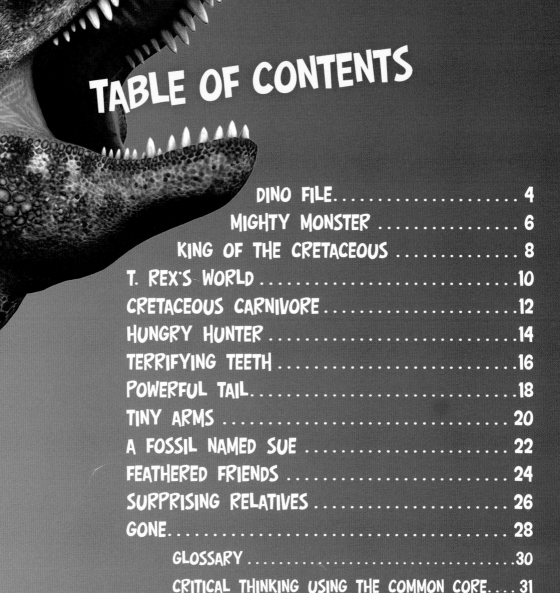

TABLE OF CONTENTS

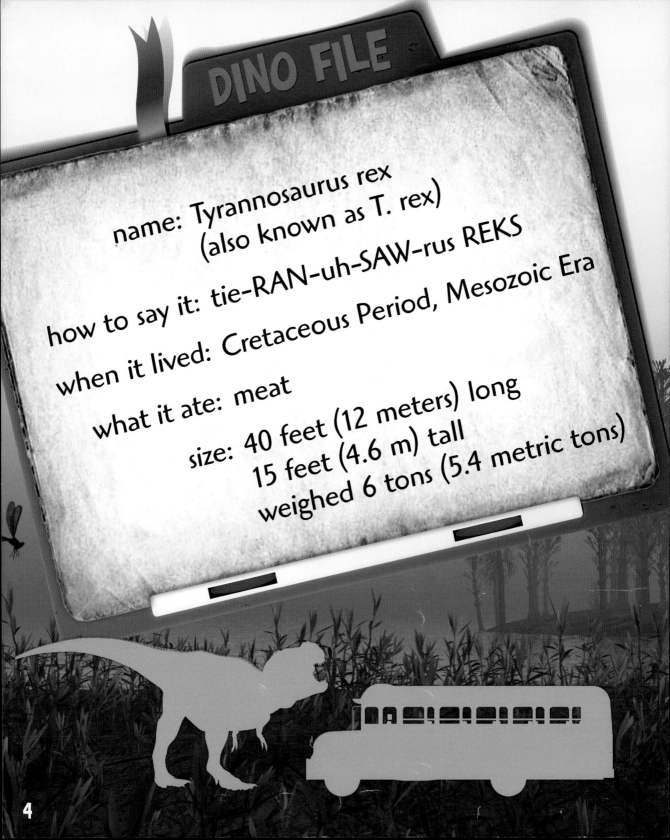

DINO FILE

name: Tyrannosaurus rex
(also known as T. rex)

how to say it: tie-RAN-uh-SAW-rus REKS

when it lived: Cretaceous Period, Mesozoic Era

what it ate: meat

size: 40 feet (12 meters) long
15 feet (4.6 m) tall
weighed 6 tons (5.4 metric tons)

Tyrannosaurus rex is one of the most famous dinosaurs. This "king of the tyrant lizards" is known for its enormous size and strength.

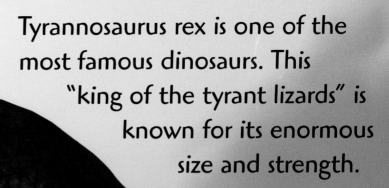

Thanks to FOSSILS

A fossil is evidence of life from the past. Fossils of things like bones, teeth, and tracks found in the earth have taught us everything we know about dinosaurs.

Let's get to know this mighty prehistoric creature!

MIGHTY MONSTER

powerful, heavy tail

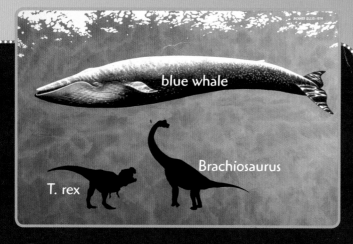

blue whale

Brachiosaurus

T. rex

T. rex may have been mighty, but it was not the biggest dinosaur. That award goes to sauropods like Brachiosaurus or Argentinosaurus. And while dinosaurs were the biggest land animals of all time, blue whales are even bigger. They are the largest animals ever known to live on Earth.

thick, heavy skull

strong upper legs

short, thick neck

short arms

7

KING OF THE CRETACEOUS

T. rex lived during the late Cretaceous Period, 68–66 million years ago. It was king of the northern continents. T. rex walked with other dinosaurs like Edmontosaurus and Triceratops.

DINOSAUR ERA

TRIASSIC	JURASSIC	CRETACEOUS	
250	200	145	66	present

millions of years ago

Other land animals in the Cretaceous Period included turtles, crocodiles, lizards, snakes, small mammals, and more birds than ever before. The sky was also busy with large and small flying reptiles called pterosaurs.

T. REX'S WORLD

During the Cretaceous Period, the continents and oceans were beginning to look more like they do today. T. rex lived in what is now western North America and eastern Asia.

Earth during Cretaceous Period

T. rex fossil site in Montana

Fossils of T. rex and its close relatives have been found in Canada and the U.S. states of Montana, South Dakota, Texas, Utah, and Wyoming.

The Cretaceous climate worldwide was very hot and wet. Sea levels were at an all-time high. Flowering plants like magnolia, ficus, and sassafras quickly grew among the evergreen forests of the Jurassic Period.

CRETACEOUS CARNIVORE

T. rex was a fierce hunter. It likely ate any meat it could find—dinosaurs, lizards, or mammals. There is even evidence to suggest that T. rexes may have eaten other T. rexes.

T. rex likely hunted plant-eating dinosaurs more often than other meat-eaters.

Scientists think that T. rex could grab up to 500 pounds (225 kilograms) with its jaws. It was so powerful it would eat its prey, bones and all!

HUNGRY HUNTER

A few scientists think T. rex was a scavenger and ate dead animals. But most agree it was a carnivore that usually hunted live prey.

Fossil discoveries support this theory:

· A Triceratops fossil was found with T. rex tooth marks.

· An Edmontosaurus fossil shows a tail that was likely wounded by a T. rex. The dinosaur healed, which tells us T. rex attacked it while it was alive.

That doesn't mean T. rex would pass up free meat from a dead animal if it found one!

T. rex's forward-facing eyes helped it see and chase moving prey.

TERRIFYING TEETH

T. rex was known for its bone-crushing teeth—it had 60 of them! (Adult humans have only 32.) T. rex lost and re-grew teeth throughout its life.

Each tooth had a job to do:

The front teeth held the prey and pulled its flesh.

The side teeth cut and ripped.

The back teeth chopped and pushed food to the back of the throat.

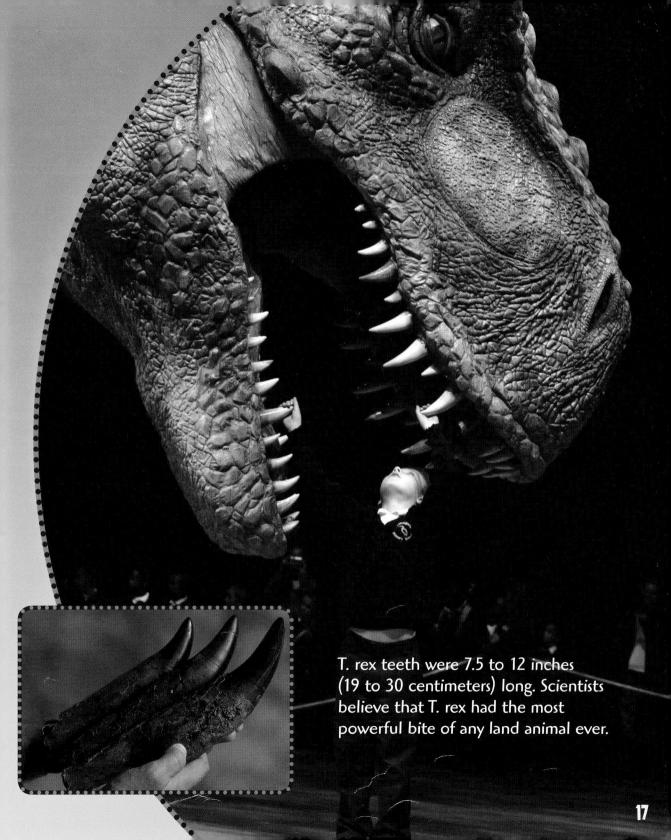

T. rex teeth were 7.5 to 12 inches (19 to 30 centimeters) long. Scientists believe that T. rex had the most powerful bite of any land animal ever.

POWERFUL TAIL

Scientists once thought T. rex stood upright like a kangaroo, with its tail dragging behind. But most fossilized dinosaur tracks show no evidence of the tail dragging.

Scientists now believe T. rex stood horizontal, like a teeter-totter. Its large, powerful tail on one end helped balance its huge head on the other end.

This horizontal position helped make T. rex one of the faster hunters of its time. It may have run as fast as 15 miles (24 kilometers) per hour.

TINY ARMS

It may seem odd that a dinosaur as big as T. rex had such small arms. They couldn't even reach its mouth. But the muscles of T. rex's arms, shoulders, and chest were very strong. Scientists know this by studying the parts of the skeleton where the muscles connected.

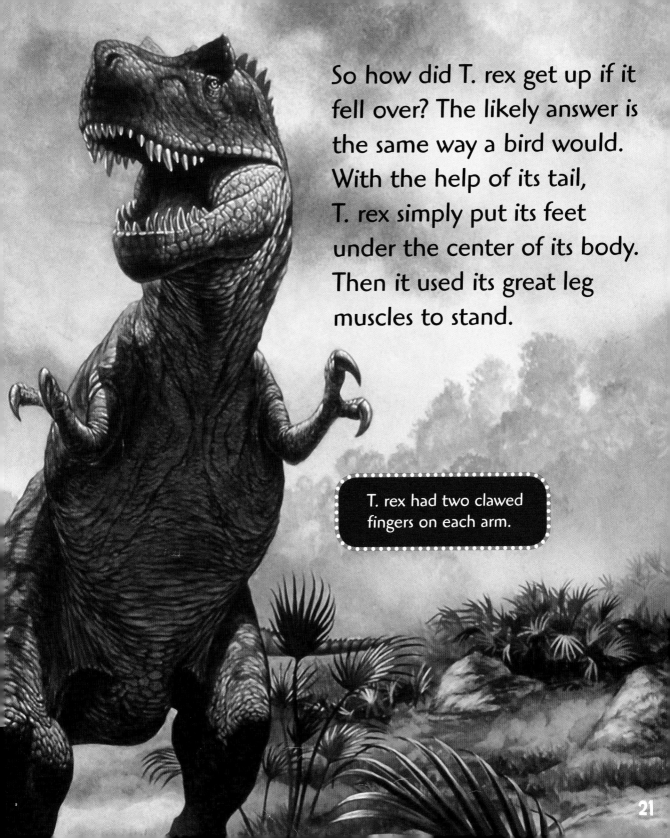

So how did T. rex get up if it fell over? The likely answer is the same way a bird would. With the help of its tail, T. rex simply put its feet under the center of its body. Then it used its great leg muscles to stand.

T. rex had two clawed fingers on each arm.

A FOSSIL NAMED SUE

The Field Museum of Natural History in Chicago is home to the largest, most complete skeleton of a T. rex ever found.

The fossil is named for Sue Hendrickson, the scientist who discovered it near Faith, South Dakota, in 1990. The skeleton has helped scientists understand much about T. rex.

Sue's skeleton weighs 3,922 pounds (1,779 kg). Her skull alone weighs 600 pounds (272 kg)!

Sue's skull shows us that T. rex had a very good sense of smell. The two parts of the brain responsible for smell were about the size of grapefruits.

FEATHERED FRIENDS

T. rex was related to some feathered dinosaurs. In fact, paleontologists think that young T. rexes had feathers but lost them as they got older. Adults were likely covered in scales.

T. rex wasn't the only dinosaur believed to have feathers. Archaeopteryx, of the late Jurassic Period, is often called the first bird.

SURPRISING RELATIVES

Bone fossils have allowed scientists to closely study the makeup of a T. rex. The studies led researchers to believe that the T. rex group and birds share a common ancestor.

Like birds, dinosaurs had hollow bones.

Most scientists believe that all dinosaurs laid eggs. Some dinosaurs even had nests, which they likely protected the same way birds do.

GONE

Tyrannosaurus rex was one of the last of the Mesozoic dinosaurs on Earth. While it isn't clear what killed the dinosaurs, one of the most common theories begins with an asteroid.

The chain of events might have looked like this:

When the asteroid crashed into Earth, it created a lot of dust, causing total darkness.

With the sun blocked, plants started to die. No plants meant no food.

Without sunlight, temperatures dropped.

Dinosaurs couldn't survive these changes, and they died out.

Mesozoic dinosaurs have been gone for about 66 million years. But we are still finding new fossils and learning new things about their lives every day.

GLOSSARY

ancestor—an animal in the past from which a new animal developed

asteroid—a large space rock that moves around the sun; asteroids are too small to be called planets

carnivore—an animal that eats meat

climate—average weather of a place throughout the year

continent—one of Earth's seven large land masses

evidence—information, items, and facts that help prove something to be true or false

extinct—no longer living; an extinct animal is one that has died out, with no more of its kind

ficus—a shrubby tree in the fig family

fossil—evidence of life from the geologic past

horizontal—flat and parallel to the ground

magnolia—a tree or large shrub that has large, fragrant flowers

Mesozoic Era—the age of dinosaurs, which includes the Triassic, Jurassic, and Cretaceous periods; when the first birds, mammals, and flowers appeared

paleontologist—a scientist who studies fossils

prey—an animal hunted by another animal for food

pterosaur—a flying animal related to dinosaurs

sassafras—a North American tree in the laurel family

sauropod—a member of a group of closely related dinosaurs with long necks, thick bodies, and long tails

scavenger—an animal that feeds on animals that are already dead

theory—an idea that brings together several hypthotheses to explain something

tyrant—a cruel ruler

CRITICAL THINKING USING THE COMMON CORE

Look at the map of Earth during the Cretaceous Period on page 10. Then find a map or globe of Earth today. How do the continents of North America and Asia look different? (Key Ideas and Details)

Read the text on page 18. Imagine a teeter-totter. Describe how the picture of the T. rex on this page looks like a teeter-totter. (Craft and Structure)

Study the flow chart on page 29. Explain in your own words how each event led to the next. (Integration of Knowledge and Ideas)

READ MORE

McCurry, Kristen. *How to Draw Incredible Dinosaurs.* Smithsonian. North Mankato, Minn.: Capstone Press, 2013.

Rockwood, Leigh. *T. Rex.* Dinosaurs Ruled! New York: PowerKids Press, 2012.

Stewart, Melissa. *Why Did T. rex Have Short Arms? And Other Questions about Dinosaurs.* Good Question. New York: Sterling Children's Books, 2014.

INTERNET SITES

FactHound offers a safe, fun way to find Internet sites related to this book. All of the sites on FactHound have been researched by our staff.

Here's all you do:

Visit *www.facthound.com*

Type in this code: 9781491408100

Check out projects, games and lots more at
www.capstonekids.com

INDEX